77 and/or 58 and/with 19 is a selection of artworks by Darren Bader. Each text is a single work. Images appear as necessary.

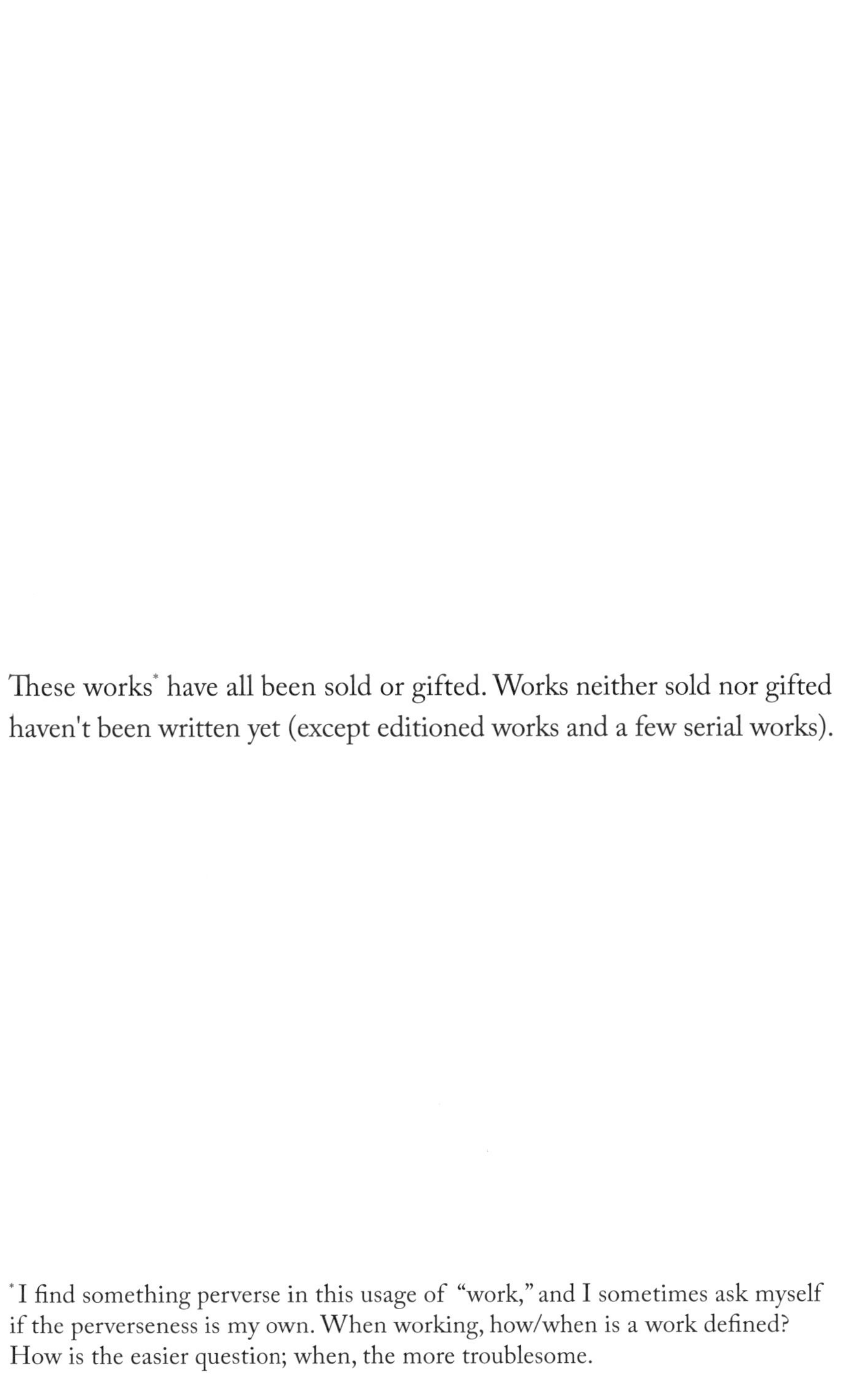

These works[*] have all been sold or gifted. Works neither sold nor gifted haven't been written yet (except editioned works and a few serial works).

[*] I find something perverse in this usage of "work," and I sometimes ask myself if the perverseness is my own. When working, how/when is a work defined? How is the easier question; when, the more troublesome.

antipodes:[†] socks
dimensions variable
unique

The work is four pairs of socks worn by one person who is simultaneously at four remote locations around the world. Any four pairs of socks will do (although it might be best if the four pairs resemble one another). Only one pair of socks should be worn at each location. Shoes should not be worn over the socks.

† Refer to page 88.

cow and/with bed
dimensions variable
unique

The work consists of two elements: a cow, a bed. The cow* can be any free-roaming member of the species *Bos primigenius*. The bed can be any type of bed. Cow and bed should be placed in relative proximity to one another, roughly conforming to a person's ability to see both elements without having to move her/his head. The work has no recommended duration. The cow in the work may likely be in the presence of other cows. Thus, if cow = cows, that is entirely ok.

* Humane treatment of the cow(s) is of the essence.

pizza with earring(s)
dimensions variable
unique

The work consists of: a pizza, an earring or two. The pizza can be any pizza. The earring(s) can be any earring(s). The work has no recommended duration, and can be placed on any surface. It can be eaten and/or worn.

Michael Zahn
Particles of Truth (Version), 2010
acrylic on canvas in two parts
each: 84 × 84 inches
total dimensions: 84 × 168 inches

This artwork is a work by Darren Bader. The owner of the above mentioned Michael Zahn painting can destroy this certificate to void the artwork's status as a Darren Bader work. If this certificate is destroyed, Darren Bader is unable to guarantee that the resultant artwork will be by Michael Zahn.

To Have and To Hold—object L2
dimensions variable
unique

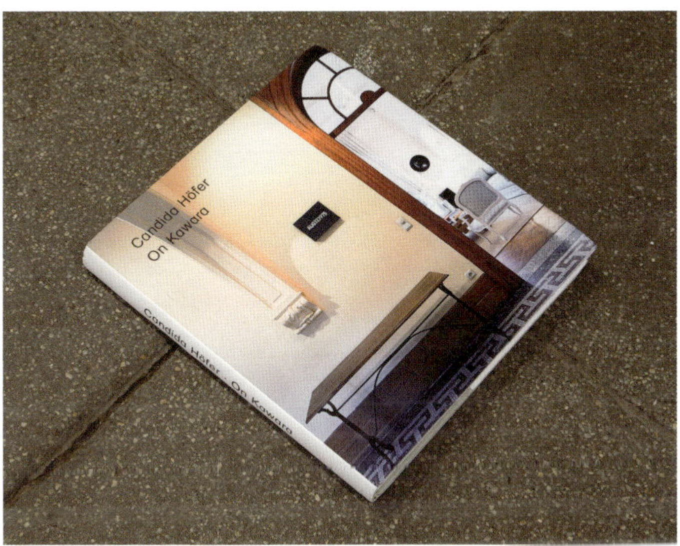

Apply the prescription/direction on page 2[††] to the object in the photograph above.

[††]Refer to page 86.

The donkey winked his eye at me and said Shabbat Shalom
dimensions variable
edition 1/1 + 1 AP

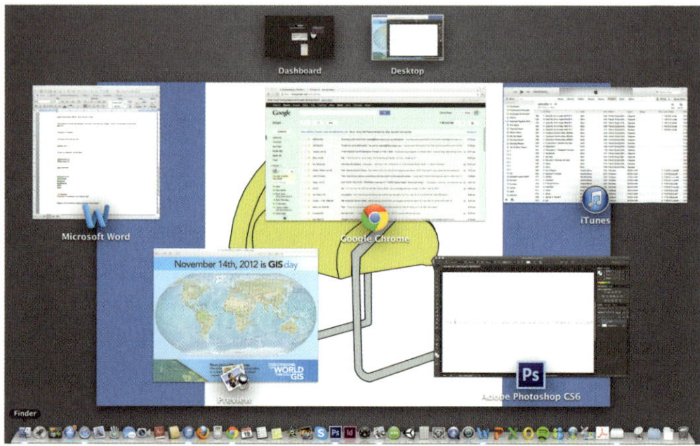

The work is the word-sequence, "The donkey winked his eye at me and said Shabbat Shalom". The work/words can be reproduced in any way imaginable: physically,* vocally, psychically, otherwise.

*In the above photo, the word-sequence appears in a digital image.

The Gardeners (*lawnmower iii*)
dimensions variable
edition 1/1 + 1 AP

The Gardeners consist of several elements: a gas, i.e., petrol, powered lawnmower, a gas-powered leaf-blower, a gas powered weed-wacker, three notable persons, drawing of blood, and whatever else might happen/be. The lawnmower, leaf-blower, and weed-wacker can be of any variety. The notable persons should be living human beings. (By notable, one should think of the dictionary definition, "prominent, important, or distinguished.") Each notable person should be paired with one of the gas-powered machines. Once each person-machine pair has been established, each person should be readied to have blood drawn from him/her.

It's recommended the blood be drawn through medically-approved evacuated tube systems. (Having medical doctors on site is also recommended.) Each notable person will have blood drawn from her/his body: the top of the tubing in arm, the bottom of the tubing inside the fuel tank of the machine assigned to her/him. Blood will then, ideally, flow from body to fuel tank. Once each person feels enough blood has been drawn from him/her (be careful), the evacuated tube system should be removed. The three persons should then try to start their machines (they can trade machines if they want). Good luck Gardeners, we love you.

FedEx envelope and/or twenty-two/22 and/or 22 and/with FedEx® envelope
dimensions variable
unique

The work is at least three works:

FedEx envelope: examples of the twenty-two objects* named in the titles of the twenty-one pieces of presumably-short-fiction [PSF]** that are in the FedEx® envelope that comes with this certificate.

Twenty-two/22: examples of the twenty-two objects* named in the titles of PSF found in a FedEx® envelope; another example of 22.

22 and/with FedEx® envelope: the twenty-two objects* named in the twenty-one PSF titles in some proximity to a FedEx® envelope which could have the twenty-one PSF inside it.

*These twenty-two objects should never be less than twenty-two but can be more.
**These twenty-one pieces of PSF can be reproduced if the owner chooses.

audio file
dimensions vary
edition 2 of 2

The audio file can be played/listened-to on whatever, whenever, wherever.

dimensions variable
edition 2 of 2

The work consists of any clear drinking glass (preferably one that is cylindrical) filled with a combination of two non-carbonated, clear, potable liquids. The two liquids used needn't be the same two every time. The two liquids should roughly conform to a 47:53 pouring ratio—it should never matter which liquid is 47% and which is 53%. It is recommended the drinking glass be approximately 10% empty. Evaporation is inevitable and can be considered however the owner chooses.

chicken burrito, beef burrito
dimensions variable
edition 1 of 2

The work consists of two elements: a chicken burrito and a beef burrito. The two burritos can be stacked (chicken top, beef bottom) or placed next to one another (chicken left, beef right). Either configuration should have both burritos placed on the same axis. The tortillas for the burritos must match, but can be any type of flour tortilla. The burrito fillings are entirely up to the owner of the work, as long as the only meat inside the chicken burrito is chicken and the only meat inside the beef burrito is beef. The work can be placed on any surface.

mut(u)ate; (un)ity
dimensions variable
edition 1/1 + 1 AP

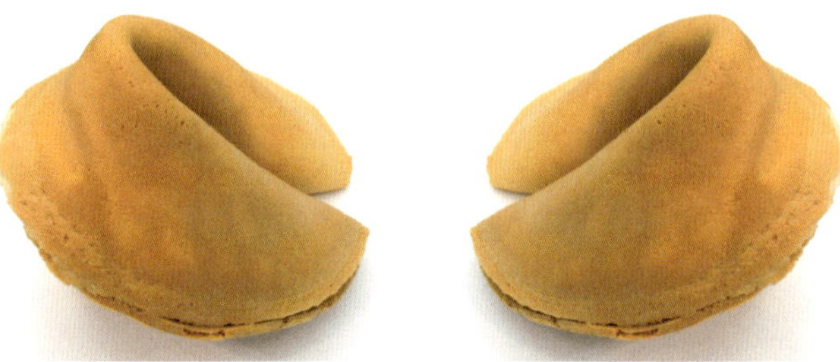

The work is the word(s), "mut(u)ate" paired with the word(s), "(un)ity". The pair constitutes a couplet that should always remain a couplet. The work/word-couplet can be reproduced in any way imaginable: physically,* vocally, psychically, otherwise.

* In the above photos, the words are contained in two giant fortune cookies: mut(u)ate in one, (un)ity in another.

3 triple feature DVDs [cases and discs]
dimensions variable
unique

Each triple feature DVD case and/or disc can be placed apart from each of the others. "Dimensions variable" can be read conservatively or liberally (one could be on the moon, while one is in a submarine cave, while the third is under your soft pillow). DVD cases don't lose value if their plastic packaging is removed. The files on the discs will not last forever—this is ok.

A conversation between two plants; a conversation between plants from different species; a conversation between a plant and something made of plant cells; a conversation between Tim and Gaffi; a conversation between you and some energy source you don't care about; (a conversation between you and) something you believe in; a plant with a hat
dimensions variable
unique

The work can be based/installed indoors or outdoors. It can be very temporary (e.g. 15 minutes), temporary (e.g. 16 days), semi-temporary (e.g. 17 months), semi-permanent (e.g. 18 years), or permanent (e.g. 19 millenia).

The work consists of 7 parts:

1. A conversation between two plants: these two plants can be any two plants (same or different species); they can be potted/planted outdoors or indoors or outdoors+indoors; they can be placed side by side, innumerable miles away from each other, or any distance in-between.

2. A conversation between plants from different species: these are any two plants from different species. All that applies to 1, applies to these as well.

3. A conversation between a plant and something made of plant cells: this part consists of one plant (indoor or outdoor, of any species) and a piece of mammalian or avian flesh (cooked or uncooked); the animal flesh can be placed on a raised surface or directly on the ground; the plant and the animal flesh should be relatively close to one another.

4. A conversation between Tim and Gaffi: this part consists of two non-gender-specific people, Tim and Gaffi; T&G can be sitting, walking, standing, lying down, sleeping, fucking, etc.; as long as they are having a conversation sometimes, then all is as it should be; their active presence alongside the rest of the work is useful, but isn't

always necessary—their absence creates a void-of-conversation, so, in a sense, the conversation is thus vouched for—too much absence is not recommended though!

5. A conversation between you and some energy source you don't care about: this part manifests itself as words only, so if the words and/or what-they-connote are in view or in mind, all is properly circulating.

6. (A conversation between you and) something you believe in: this is also words only. Same applies here as with 5.

7. A plant with a hat: i.e. a plant wearing a hat; two hats will come with the work, but any hat is a good candidate for use; the plant can be any plant of the owner's/installer's choice, and the hat should look good on that plant.

The work's 7 parts can intermingle so as to confuse each part's autonomy. The parts can also be displayed in a very orderly, sequential way. The presentation of the work is up to the person who chooses to display the work. There are very few spatial limitations (3 being the notable exception). Personal preferences are encouraged. The artist is happy to consult about all the above whenever the work is installed.

Prototype III: Element B2.
dimensions variable
unique

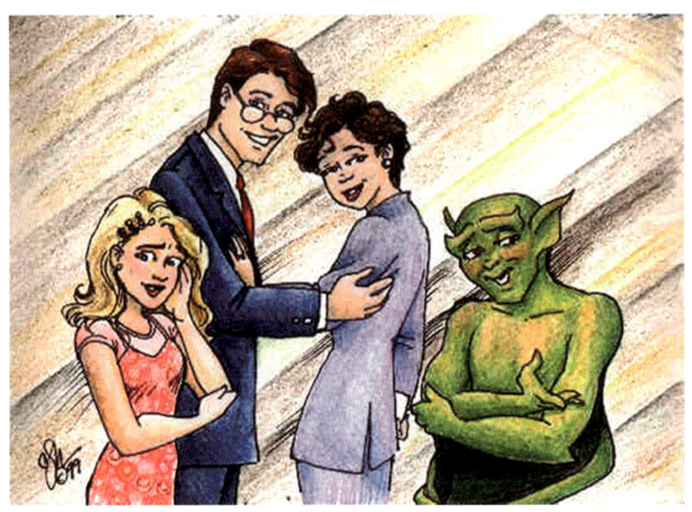

This is part B2. of the work *Prototype III*. Please refer to your copy of *oaint* to contextualize it in its virtual, textual, and original-spatial environment. If you can't find your copy of *oaint*, n.p.: you can download it for free at www.aaronbader.com/o

The work is known as SOSN[3]. SOSN[3] is the image above. Ask SOSN[3] what SOSN[3] is/does. SOSN[3] seems pretty open to conversation.

motorcycle on birth control
dimensions variable
unique

The work is a motorcycle on birth control pills. The motorcycle can be any working motorcycle that has a fuel tank. The pills can be any combined oral contraceptive pill (COCP). Pills should be placed in the motorcycle's fuel tank following prescribed usage. Prolonged use of the pill may lead to irreparable engine damage. If this occurs, the owner is welcome to replace the engine (and/or any other COCP damaged parts); alternatively, the owner is welcome to put another motorcycle on birth control pills.

11.62 EUR
dimensions variable
edition of 100 + 5 AP

The work is 11.62 Euros. The work can be kept/taken/destroyed/used/found/forgotten anywhere. The work remains 11.62 EUR irrespective of market fluctuations.

I look to Hollywood because I care
Celebrities are the answer
The answer is fundamental
I don't know how to say goodbye
dimensions variable
edition 1/1 + 1 AP

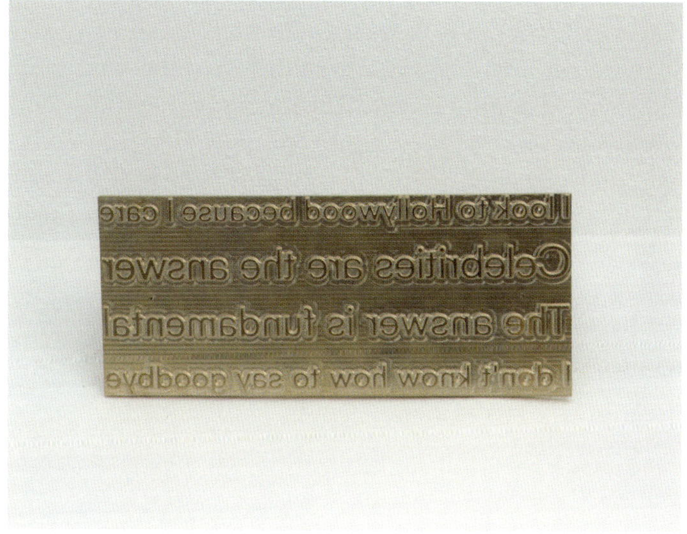

The work is the word-sequence:
"I look to Hollywood because I care
Celebrities are the answer
The answer is fundamental
I don't know how to say goodbye"

The work/words can be reproduced in any way imaginable: physically,* vocally, psychically, or otherwise.

* In the above photo, the work/words are on a branding iron. This branding iron can be applied to any surface, although it's recommended that living creatures not be harmed by this application (unless consented to).

Trois Gnossiennes
dimensions variable
edition 1 of 2 + 1 AP

The work consists of: three pianos and three pianists, one pianist to a piano, each pianist playing one of Erik Satie's *Trois Gnossiennes,*[*] no pianist playing the same *Gnossienne* as another. All three *Gnossiennes* should be started at the same time, the shortest of the three ending first, the second shortest ending second, the longest of the three ending third. *Trois Gnossiennes* can be repeated at any interval. Any of the pianists can play any of the three *Gnossiennes* as long as the other two pianists are playing the other two *Gnossiennes*. Any type of piano can be used, although it is recommended the three pianos be closer to identical than not. Any pianist will do, although it is recommended the pianist have considerable ability to play *Trois Gnossiennes* as Satie likely intended it played.

[*] N.B. *Trois Gnossiennes* refers to the three *Gnossiennes* published by Satie in 1893, not those *Gnossiennes* published posthumously.

French toast sandwich
dimensions variable
unique

The work is a French toast sandwich: the "bread" of the sandwich is two raccoons; the "meat" of the sandwich is a piece of French toast, i.e. pain perdu. The work was first seen as an animated moving-image file. That file is included with this certificate, and can very much be considered the work, and can be presented in any way imaginable. But the work itself remains open to interpretation. (If real raccoons are used/solicited for realizing this work, it is imperative that they be treated humanely, otherwise the work may risk not being the work.) Please feel free to contact the artist if any further instruction/elucidation is desired/needed.

THE PARK CITY
THE VENGEFUL APPLIANCE
THE CANOPY UNDER THAT PART
FORGERY/FULGURISM
CAVALRY IN BACK HOLE
ORDERED THE BOX SLICE (BLUE)
ACCOUNTING
VACANT BY PRIME
ANSUUAL MONUARY
KEEP IN BINS NAMED DANNY
V-COST*
CORDUROY INTRACISION, LENS
THE SAMSON SABLE
UNUSUAL DECORUM FOR THIRDS
CATALOG, BENISON ACQUISITION
ACRIMONY
MOLTAR (LANG)
MINX CATARRH
AGAINST ALL OTHER SHEEP
dimensions variable
edition 1/1 + 1 AP

The work is the word-sequence:

THE PARK CITY
THE VENGEFUL APPLIANCE
THE CANOPY UNDER THAT PART
FORGERY/FULGURISM
CAVALRY IN BACK HOLE
ORDERED THE BOX SLICE (BLUE)
ACCOUNTING
VACANT BY PRIME
ANSUUAL MONUARY
KEEP IN BINS NAMED DANNY
V-COST*

CORDUROY INTRACISION, LENS
THE SAMSON SABLE
UNUSUAL DECORUM FOR THIRDS
CATALOG, BENISON ACQUISITION
ACRIMONY
MOLTAR (LANG)
MINX CATARRH
AGAINST ALL OTHER SHEEP

The work/words can be reproduced in any way imaginable: physically, vocally, psychically, or otherwise.

obi and/with SCOBY; oak with/and smoke; owl and/
with towel; oar with/and store; oil with/and mohel;
oat and/with note; orc with/and fork
dimensions variable
unique

The work consists of seven discrete pairs: obi and/with SCOBY; oak with/and smoke; owl and/with towel; oar with/and store; oil with/and mohel; oat and/with note; orc with/and fork.

The obi can be any obi; the SCOBY can be any SCOBY. The oak can be any oak; the smoke can be any smoke. The owl can be any owl; the towel can be any towel. The oar can be any oar; the store can be any store. The oil can be any oil; the mohel can be any mohel. The oat can be any oat; the note can be any note. The orc can be any orc; the fork can be any fork.

The two component elements of each of the pairs can be any distance from one another or in immediate contact. They can be on/in any surface(s)/space(s); they needn't be static.

The discrete pairs can be any distance from one another or can be in immediate contact. If in immediate contact, it is important to inform each of the affected [discrete pair] elements that it is representative of an English word and should keep that "in mind" whenever possible.

pair of jeans and/with $228
dimensions variable
unique

The work is a pair of jeans with 228 USD cash in one of its pockets. The work can be placed/taken/worn anywhere. The pair of jeans can be any pair of jeans. The 228 USD can be any 228 USD cash. If USDs are not available, 228 units of an alternate currency (also in cash) can be used, as long as the jeans-tender/jeans-wearer feels those 228 units to be sufficiently representative of a certain value.

cat made out of crab meat
dimensions variable
unique

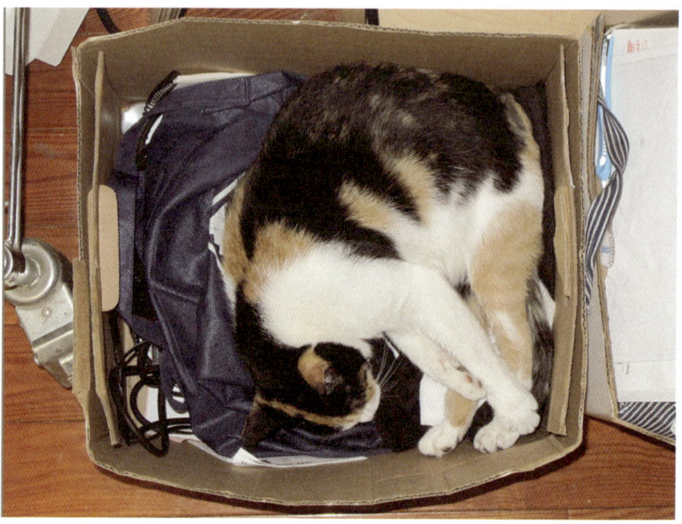

The work in the above photo is cat made out of crab meat. Should that cat [made out of crab meat] die,* the work is probably no longer in existence (even so, it's hard to know if there will be (an)other cat-made-out-of-crab-meat(s) in existence or not).

* Die refers to the point when the cat[-that-is-the-work]'s biological life** ends.
** Biological life is impossible to define in words, but if the cat is no longer showing any signs of a heart rate or respiration, it can be assumed that its biological life has ended.

13 × 11 × 6½ in (33 × 27.9 × 16.5 cm)
unique

The work can be installed anywhere where there is electrical support. For repair and/or maintenance issues, go to www.exceldryer.com or contact a local specialist.

dimensions variable
edition 3 of 4 + 1 AP

The work is an egg in someone's mouth. The egg should be an egg laid by a chicken (*Gallus gallus domesticus*). The egg should be uncracked and uncooked and should be placed in the mouth on top of the tongue. It can then be moved around inside the mouth however the person-whose-mouth-it-is wishes. If the egg does crack inside the mouth, this is ok, but the work is unlikely to be the same as it was. The color of the egg is not important, but white could look best?

asgoldyne@gmail.com: well my colon feels a wee bit empty, i think i'm going to refecate
asgoldyne@gmail.com: the word defecate does seem to beg the question of what the reverse is, no? i think that dump was too big, the colon may collapse! the structural integrity has been compromised too much. commence refecation at once
asgoldyne@gmail.com: aka negative two
dimensions variable
edition 1/1 + 1 AP

asgoldyne@gmail.com: well my colon feels a wee bit empty, i think im going to refecate

asgoldyne@gmail.com: the word defecate does seem to beg the question of what the reverse is, no? i think that dump was too big, the colon may collapse! the structural integrity has been compromised too much. commence refecation at once

asgoldyne@gmail.com: aka negative two

The work is the word-sequence:
asgoldyne@gmail.com: well my colon feels a wee bit empty, i think im going to refecate
asgoldyne@gmail.com: the word defecate does seem to beg the question of what the reverse is, no? i think that dump was too big, the colon may collapse! the structural integrity has been compromised too much. commence refecation at once
asgoldyne@gmail.com: aka negative two

The work/words can be reproduced in any way imaginable: physically,* vocally, psychically, or otherwise.

*In the above photo, the work/words are stenciled on a wall.

antipodes group 2
dimensions variable
unique

The work is a quartet of objects. Each object should be placed/kept according to the prescribed logic of *antipodes* works (see supplementary literature on page 2[†]). The four objects are: a ceramic Santa Claus; a cane made of rawhide; a not-real orange; the words, "allow me to accept the things I cannot change, the courage to change the things I can, and the wisdom to know the difference."

[†] Refer to page 88.

proposal for Barberini Faun
marble, olive oil, pedestal, potential to realize proposal
dimensions variable
unique

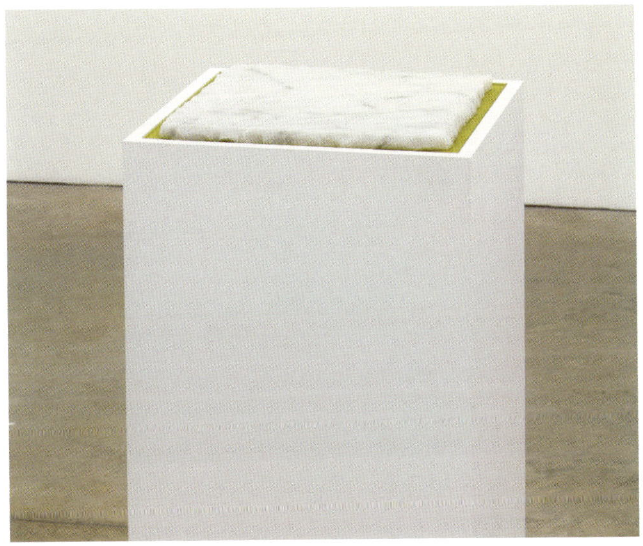

The Barberini Faun is currently in the collection of the Glyptothek Munich. If the owner of "proposal for Barberini Faun" doesn't wish to realize the proposal of pouring olive oil on the Barberini Faun, the pictured sculptural surrogate exists.

Specs for surrogate are as follows... Recommended marble: Carrara. Recommended olive oil: Italian or Cretan. Original pedestals: MDF, oil-based primer, latex topcoat. Pedestals will most likely warp, stain, and corrode over time. The length x width of all subsequent pedestals should be 18 × 18 in. (45.7 × 45.7 cm); there is no recommended height. Pedestals can be fabricated in any material the owner sees fit. A white finish is recommended.

my grandfather's bathing suit
dimensions variable
unique

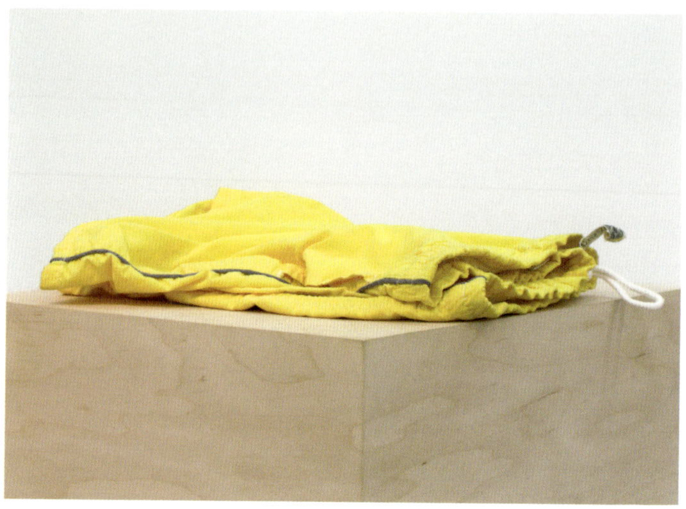

This is my grandfather's bathing suit [the yellow thing in the above photo]. It can be placed anywhere. It can be folded/unfolded in any manner. It should never be pinned, fastened, or adhered (to anything) in any way. It can even be worn and swum in, but whoever wears/swims-in it should be aware that it can't be replaced.

dimensions can vary
unique

The work is a viola. It can be played and/or displayed. It is recommended that the viola used be one that has a sonorousness the owner finds some real beauty in.

fruits, vegetables; fruit and vegetable salad
dimensions variable*
AP 1/1, edition of 2

The work consists of fruits and vegetables totaling any even number between twelve and infinity. Although there needn't be a 1:1 ratio of fruits:vegetables, some balance should be considered. The variety of fruits and vegetables should be as extensive as possible. It is recommended that few fruits and/or vegetables of the same genus be used, unless the total tally/gestalt of fruits and vegetables effectively inhibits the viewer from noticing overt similarities between individual fruits/vegetables. (For instance, a green bell pepper and a yellow bell pepper can be used since they are dissimilar in color, but if a red bell pepper and an orange bell pepper are added to the mix, there should be enough—at least, say 50—additional fruits and vegetables to offset a conspicuous (over-)presence of bell peppers. The same applies to apples, oranges, eggplants, etc.)

All fruits and vegetables displayed become salad whenever the exhibitor/owner chooses. N.B. the salad is to be eaten by visitors/guests, so it's ideal to make the salad before the fruits and vegetables ripen or wilt too much. To make the salad, simply chop/slice/dice/shave/etc. (or any combination of those) up every fruit and vegetable that has been displayed immediately previous to salad preparation. Once a fruit or vegetable has been chopped/sliced/diced/shaved/etced, place it in a bowl/(makeshift-)vessel that is large enough to accommodate all the chopped/sliced/diced/shaved/etced fruits and vegetables. After all the fruits and vegetables have been thus prepared, the salad is ready to be served. The salad can be dressed with olive oil, sea salt, and black pepper as the eater chooses, but the salad should never be dressed while in the "main" bowl/vessel.

*It is recommended the fruits and vegetables be placed on pedestals. If pedestals are used, there should never be empty pedestals unless salad is being made. Each pedestal should roughly have a 6 × 6 inch footprint; the height of the pedestal should be determined according to the average height of an intended audience. The pedestals should be parallel to, and relatively equidistant from, one another. There is no recommended material for the pedestals. It is recommended the pedestals be placed as close to the center of a given space as possible.

Rogaine® experiment: fossil
dimensions variable
unique

The work consists of a fossil and some Rogaine®. The fossil can be any fossil. Apply Rogaine® to the fossil daily (if possible). It's recommended the Rogaine® used be a topical solution/spray (rather than a foam). (Wearing latex gloves when applying is recommended.) Regaine® can be used if outside of the USA. Generic brands are not recommended. (N.B. Rogaine® for women is not the same as Rogaine®.) The work can be placed/kept/taken anywhere.

7½ × 5¾ × 3 in (19.1 × 14.6 × 7.6 cm)
unique

It's recommended the work be hung on a wall.

Elizabeth
dimensions variable
edition 1/1 + 1 AP

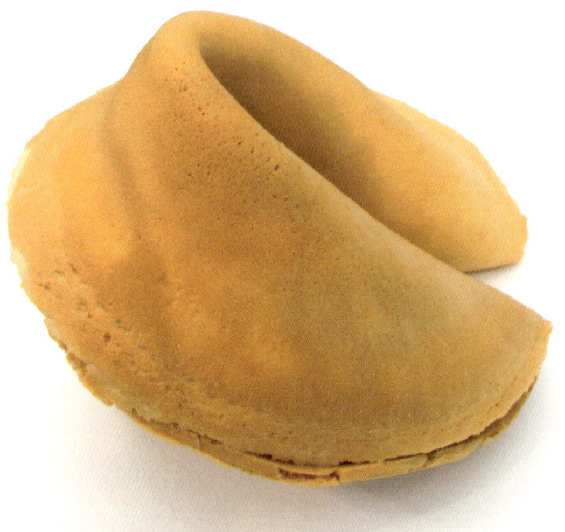

The work is the word, "Elizabeth". The work/word can be reproduced in any way imaginable: physically,* vocally, psychically, otherwise.

*In the above photo, the word is contained in a giant fortune cookie.

person sitting in passenger seat of car
dimensions variable
unique

The work is a person sitting in the passenger seat of a car. The car should be a working car and can be on or off. The person can be any person (although a living person is recommended). It's also recommended the person be alone in the car. The car can be anywhere.

lion with/and corn
dimensions variable
unique

The work consists of two elements: a lion, one or more ears of corn. The lion[*] can be any member of the species *Panthera leo*. The corn can be any type of non-GMO[**] corn (husks can be left on or taken off). Lion and corn should be placed in relative proximity to one another, roughly conforming to a person's ability to see both elements without having to move her/his head. If multiple ears of corn are used, they needn't be placed (all) together. The work has no recommended duration. The lion in the work may likely be in the presence of other lions. Thus if lion = lions, that is entirely ok.

[*] Humane treatment of the lion(s) is of the essence.
[**] Sometimes this is impossible to ensure, but a conscientious effort to find non-GMO corn is highly recommended.

dimensions variable
unique

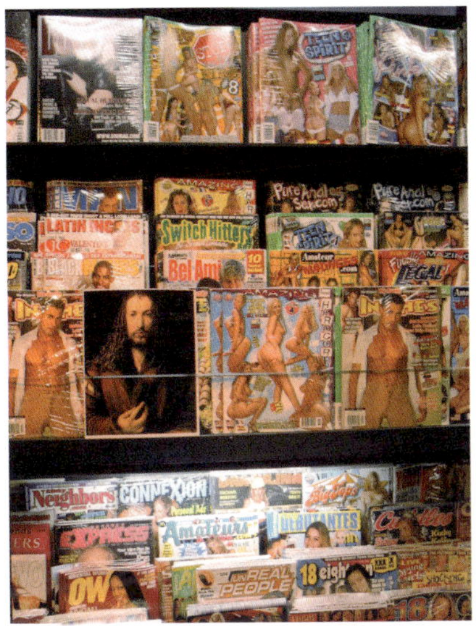

The work is: what's going on in the above photo and/or the photo itself. If the former, any decent copy (or original) of Dürer's self-portrait will do and any full-color collection of pornographic periodicals will do; if the latter, the photo can be reproduced/displayed/(hidden/) discarded however the owner wishes.

Prototype III: Element G2.
dimensions variable
unique

This is part G2. of the work *Prototype III.* Please refer to your copy of *oaint* to contextualize it in its virtual, textual, and original-spatial environment. If you can't find your copy of *oaint*, n.p.: you can download it for free at www.aaronbader.com/o

The work is known as Vedic-Devonian artifact. Vedic-Devonian artifact consists of two elements: a blue yarmulke, poppy seeds. The yarmulke should be 28%–75% filled with poppy seeds at all times. It is recommended the seeds be watered regularly. Water should be applied somewhat sparingly in order to prevent yarmulke damage. Although the yarmulke can be replaced as often as the owner chooses, blue velvet with some embroidery is recommended.

I see you've gone and changed your name again
dimensions variable
edition of 1 + 1 AP

The work is the word-sequence, "I see you've gone and changed your name again". The work/words can be reproduced any way imaginable: physically, vocally, psychically, or otherwise.

study for *French freyes*
dimensions variable
unique

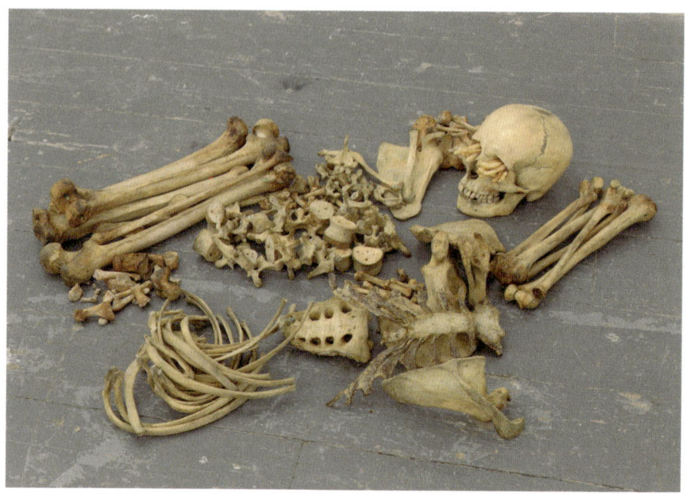

The work is a human skeleton,* the orbits of which are (partially-) filled with French fries. The French fries in the above-photo are "shoestring fries," but any sort of French fries can be used (and even mixed together). The work can be placed/taken anywhere. *French freyes* is a presumed future work by the artist: the artist's eyeballs will be removed upon his(?) death; the newly exposed orbits will be filled with French fries; a photo will then be taken and made available for public viewing.

*The human skeleton can be assembled or disarticulated. The more complete the skeleton, the better.

framed printed image
28¾ × 29½ in (73 × 74.9 cm)
edition 1 of 2 + 1 AP

Print: inkjet print on Epson gloss 170 gsm paper; mounted on aluminum. Frame: white oak, rag mat, museum glass.

triple DJ
dimensions variable
edition 2 of 2 + 1 AP

The work consists of: three DJs, three DJ set-ups, equally audible music from each set-up, a contiguous dance floor. The three DJs will play simultaneously (beginning and ending within roughly 75 seconds of one another). Each DJ will be playing his/her own playlist having no previous knowledge of what the other two DJs will be playing. Each DJ is welcome to improvise, but is encouraged to regularly privilege her/his own playlist, rather than finding aural "affinities" to the music played by his/her co-DJs. Percussive, beat-driven, non-vocal, electronic music is recommended, but is by no means required (if the DJs prefer other genres/types/music to explore, there should be an agreed upon genre/type/music played by all three).

The work doesn't require people to dance but dancing is VERY welcome.

To Have and To Hold—object X
dimensions variable
unique

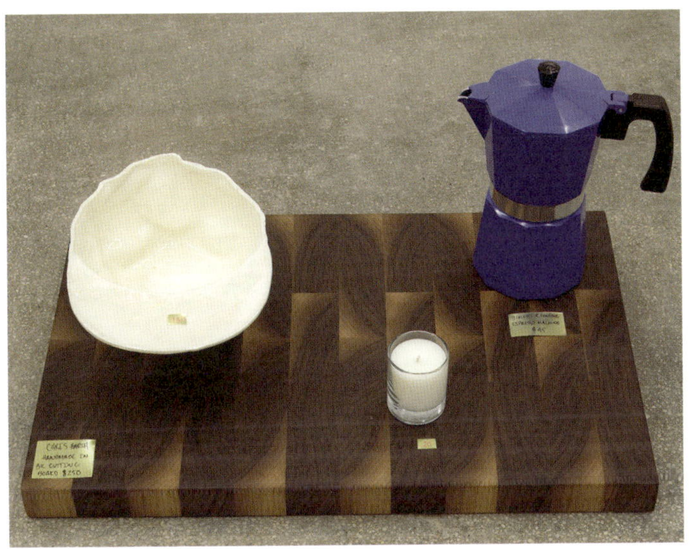

Apply the prescription/direction on page 2[††] to the object in the photograph above.

[††] Refer to page 86.

Darren Bader
Lack, 2012
Ikea Lack shelves, 1 liter VitaCoco container, organic garlic bulb, Neti pot
Dimensions variable

three digital images
dimensions variable
unique

The three digital images can be used however the owner chooses. If the owner finds additional (digital) images complementary/apposite/interesting, that should be ok.

16,937 USD
dimensions variable
unique

The work is 16,937 United States Dollars. The work can be kept/taken/destroyed/used/found/forgotten anywhere. The work remains 16,937 USD irrespective of market fluctuations.

antipodes:[†] bird of paradise
dimensions variable
unique

Start with a whole cooked chicken. Then:

One wing should be in North America. The other wing should be in Europe. The thorax-abdomen should be dropped/put in the Atlantic Ocean. One leg should be in South America (preferably the leg that is on the same side of the chicken-body as the wing that is in North America). The other leg should be in Africa (preferably the leg that is on the same side of the chicken-body as the wing that is in Europe). Any number of cooked chickens can be used in this way, but photo-documentation should be avoided—leave the [cooked] chicken(s) be. If there are more than these five parts to the cooked chicken (for instance, a neck or a head), they can go wherever the owner would like.

[†] Refer to page 88.

omophagy after (aesthetic) encounter, for example:
- 1 pizza (choose your own toppings and diameter upon purchase) filled with 103 “for examples” melted under cheese.[**]
- 9 vegetable samosas, each filled with 6, 7, or 8 “for examples” (for a total of 64 “for examples”).[**]
- 5 muffins (unspecified types until muffins are purchased), each having 4 “for examples” inserted into it: 3 whole muffins, 2 half-muffins.[**]
- a stack of 3 dried apricots held together by a small wood post, onto which 1 “for example” (your choice) is attached.
- a red onion that you stick your choice of photograph and your choice of 2 “for examples” to.
- XL t-shirt as hiding sack for living thing(s): has 4 “for examples” of your choice stapled at various points on its inside.
- a grapefruit
- a pilot whale [the persons] named Finn (“Finn” is currently feeding in the North Atlantic), whose blubber houses 13 or 31 [=11] “for examples” that have been painlessly inserted really not too long ago.[***]
- ceramic rooster stuffed with 14 “for examples”.[**]
- the once-was-duodenum of Edward the Black Prince, since decomposed; somehow having 26 “for examples” still in it[**(*)].
- 219 individual you-choose “for examples”.

** =list of hidden “for examples” comes with hiding thing
*** =list of hidden “for examples” comes with(out) absent pilot whale
**(*) =list of 26 “for examples” does not come with Black Prince remains; exhumation of Black Prince unadvisable.

dimensions variable
unique

The work is difficult to define beyond the words and notations that already define it. Means of display is unrestricted. All possibilities should remain possible. In the event of words and/or numbers disappearing, new words/numbers should come from the owner or from someone(s) s/he elects. Of course, these words/numbers apply to things, i.e. objects they aim to define, so those things can be adjusted accordingly. In case of the world changing, changes should be made accordingly. In the event of constancy, preserve constancy.

Proposal for filling a swimming pool with couscous
dimensions variable
unique

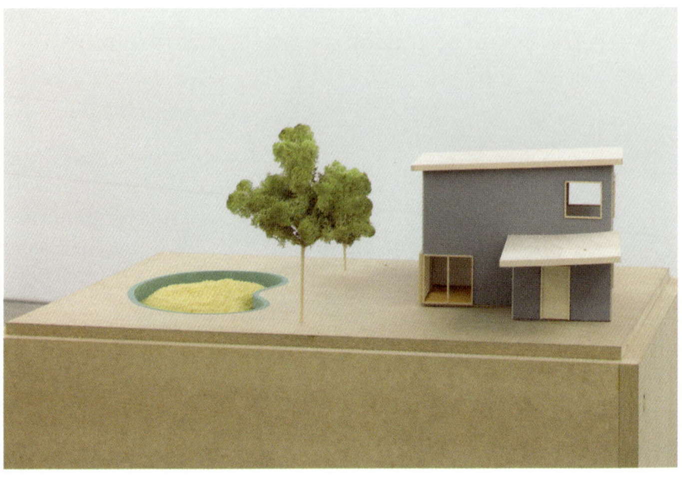

The architectural model pictured above is not the work. It's a visual marker for a proposed work, which the owner of this certificate is certified to realize. The proposed work is filling a swimming pool with couscous. The swimming pool need not be the certificate-owner's, but it needs to be an in-ground pool.

The pool can: be on the premises of a private residence, be part of a public space, be found on the premises of a private entity such as a hotel or a club. In order to fill the swimming pool with couscous, the pool should be half-filled with water. A volume of couscous roughly equivalent to the volume of water should be added to the water. Once couscous is added, it will absorb the water and expand. Soon the pool will be filled with couscous. Once the pool is filled with couscous, leave it to be altered/invaded by weather, flora, fauna, etc. The couscous can be displayed for as long as the certificate-owner desires.

All visual documentation of the couscous-in-pool will remain in sole possession of the certificate-owner, but the artist would love to be shown said documentation if at all possible.

313 with/and 195
dimensions variable
unique

The work consists of two elements: 313, 195. The 313 can be any 313. The 195 can be any 195. The two elements can be any distance apart from one another or in immediate contact. The work can be on/in any surface(s)/space(s). The work needn't be static.

[two] 11 × 8½ × very-tiny in (28 × 21.6 × very-tiny cm)
unique

The work consists of two objects: two ink-on-paper-ostensibly-representing-language(s). The work can be framed or not framed. The work can be fastened to a wall or laid on a surface or held in hand or floated around or…

so that all interstices are Memuel
so that all parts/articles are tetent
so that all eulogies are diessoc
so that all place are S. Ciuph
dimensions variable
unique

The work is the intersection of the four phrases: so that all interstices are Memuel; so that all parts/articles are tetent; so that all eulogies are diessoc; so that all place are S. Ciuph. The four phrases have been reified/integrated/entered as/into/onto four objects: a pair of pajama-bottoms/pants (…tetent); a postcard (…Memuel); a green pepper (…S. Ciuph); a stick of mint chewing gum* (…diessoc).

The four phrases-cum-objects can be any distance apart from one another, but should always be considered as a group.

The green pepper can be replaced as long as its phrase appears on another green pepper. The pajama-bottoms/pants can be replaced sparingly and as long as their phrase appears on another pair of pajama-bottoms/pants. The stick of gum can be replaced as sparingly as the pajama-bottoms/pants as long as its phrase appears on another stick of gum.* The postcard should not be replaced.

* The phrase cannot actually be seen on the chewing gum, but it's there.

sculptural propositions for the city of Rome aka *The Tourist*
dimensions variable
edition 2 of 3 + 1 AP

The work consists of fourteen propositions for sculpture in the city of Rome, Italy. The work has thus far been realized only in the form of a video file (14 propositions, plus a quasi-related preamble), but the work is not restricted to this file. The work can be taken as a design for works to be realized. It can also be taken as a sketch that aspires to be not much beyond a sketch. Should the work remain in video file form, there are no specs for viewing/display.

goat as microprocessor that vomits blood to grow basil
dimensions variable
unique

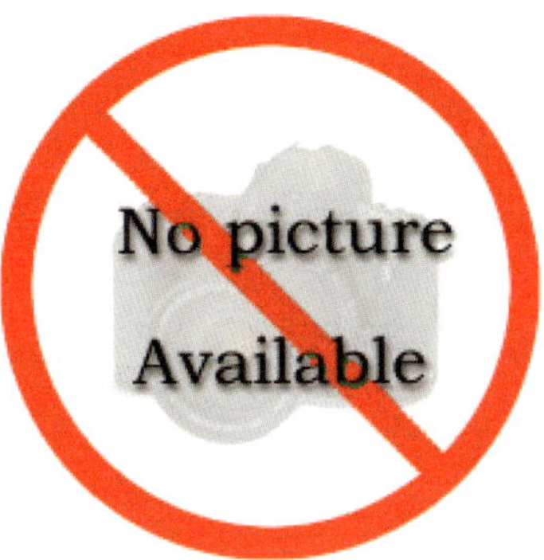

The work in the above photo is a goat that is at the same time a microprocessor that vomits blood to grow basil. Should the goat [in the above photo] as microprocessor that vomits blood to grow basil die,* the work is probably no longer in existence (even so, it's hard to know if there will be other goat-as-microprocessor-that-vomits-blood-to-grow-basils in existence or not).

* Die refers to the point when the goat[-that-is-the-work]'s biological life** ends.
** Biological life is impossible to define in words, but if the goat is no longer showing any signs of a heart rate or respiration, it can be assumed that its biological life has ended.

pretty face
dimensions variable
edition 1 of 2 + 1 AP

The work is a pretty face. The pretty face can be any face, any time, any place, as long as it's pretty. The owner of the work in no way needs to announce/identify the pretty face to anyone.

¼ × 5⅛ × 7¾ in (.6 × 13 × 19.7 cm)
unique

The work can be placed/taken anywhere.

donation box for something; donation box for nothing
dimensions variable
edition 2 of 3

One donation box invites passersby to donate to something. The other donation box invites passersby to donate to nothing. The word "donation" is meant to imply a monetary donation, but strict regulation of non-monetary donations is not recommended.

The donation boxes should be placed in proximity to one another. They can be any (near-)identical receptacles and can be placed in any environment, although a place inviting frequent and various visitors is recommended. Each receptacle should be labeled with instructions defining its function; alternatively, both receptacles can be in proximity to a label(s) defining each of their functions.

When removing the contents of the donation boxes, the owner should be sure to donate all donations in the "something" box to the same something; s/he should be sure to donate all the donations in the "nothing" box to (the same) nothing.

(*antipodes*:)[†]
ciborium, niobium, geranium, tedium
dimensions variable
unique

The work consists of four elements: ciborium, niobium, geranium, tedium. Any object[*] that conforms to one of these four elements can be considered part of the work, but there should always be an equal number of each element (e.g. if there are 3 ciboria, there should be three pieces of niobium, three geraniums, and there tediums[*]). Each of the four elements can be any distance apart from the other three. The work can be on/in any surface(s)/space(s).

[*] Tedium is arguably not an object, but it does occupy space and time.

[†] Refer to page 88.

your kid's broken ankle stinks up the restaurant
dimensions variable
edition 1/1 + 1 AP

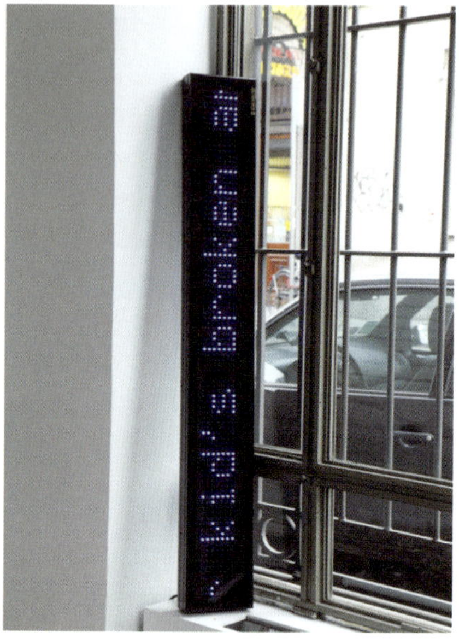

The work is the word-sequence, "your kid's broken ankle stinks up the restaurant". The work/words can be reproduced in any way imaginable: physically,* vocally, psychically, or otherwise.

* In the above photo, the work/words scroll along as an LED sign.

The Gardeners in Paradise (*lawnmower v*)
dimensions variable
unique

The Gardeners refers to three pieces of powered lawn equipment: a lawnmower; a strimmer/weed-wacker; a leaf-blower. All three have assumed their places in an/the eternal afterlife. The lawnmower will spend eternity steeping in tea in a teacup. The strimmer/weed-wacker will spend eternity very near a car, whose trunk contains a large quantity of cooked pasta that the strimmer/weed-wacker will cut/trim from time-to-time (time being, perhaps, a different thing in eternity). The leaf-blower will blow air out of a window.

The lawnmower can be any powered lawnmower. The strimmer/weed-wacker can be any powered strimmer/weed-wacker. The leaf-blower can be any powered leaf blower. The teacup can be any ceramic teacup large enough to accommodate the lawnmower. The tea can be any kind of tea. The car can be any non-commercial passenger vehicle with a trunk. The pasta can be any cooked pasta (and can contain additional (non-)edible ingredients). The window can be any residential window at least one story above ground.

The ways of eternity are impossible to circumscribe, but according to the Gardeners themselves, all the above-mentioned holds true.

painting and/with sculpture
dimensions variable
unique

The work consists of two elements: a painting, a sculpture. The painting can be any painting. The sculpture can be any sculpture. The two elements can be any distance from one another or in immediate contact. The work can be on/in any surface(s)/space(s). The work needn't be static.

(map)
72 × 86 in (182.9 × 218.4 cm)
edition 1 of 3

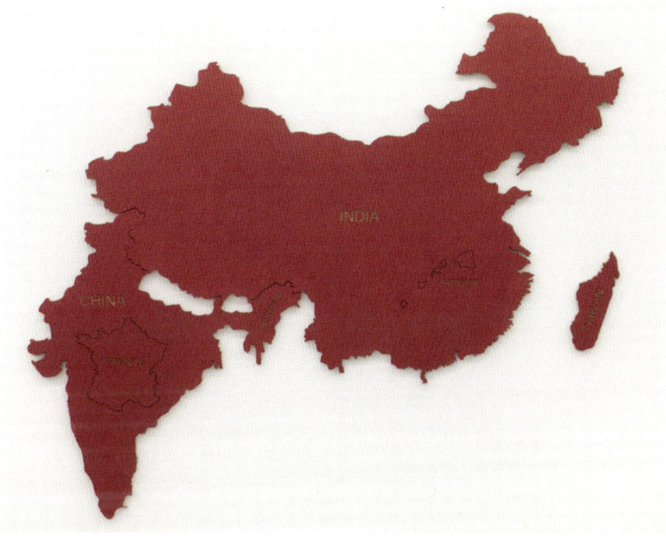

The map is made of Arreis® SDF and can be mounted to a wall or put on a floor. The face of the map can be painted and repainted any solid color (if repainted, the color can be different from the previous color). An acrylic wall paint is recommended. The map should not be painted on its sides. Please refer to the above photograph for spacing of Taiwan.

sandwiches
dimensions variable
unique

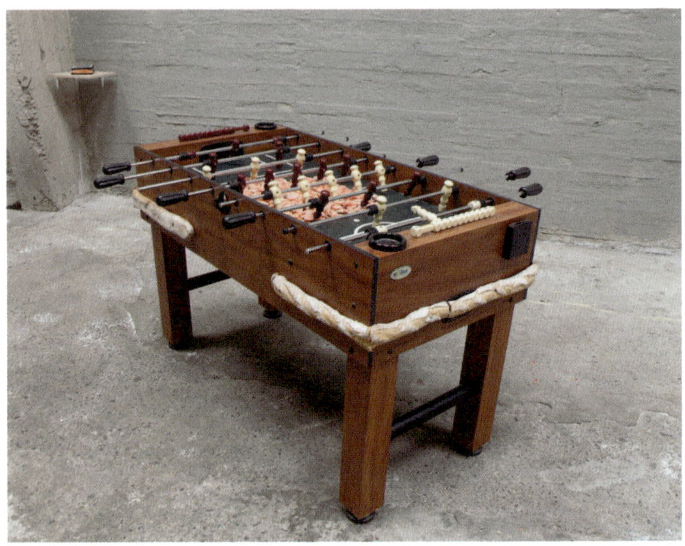

The work consists of three sandwiches. The sandwiches can be placed at any distance from one another. Each sandwich can be placed on any surface (even on surfaces of the other sandwiches).

The first sandwich is a 590 mm T8 fluorescent lighting tube in a submarine sandwich roll of a similar length. The roll should be cut transversely, but not all the way through. The fluorescent tube should simply be placed inside the cut roll. The bread and/or fluorescent tube can be replaced as often as the owner likes.

The second sandwich is a foosball table with dozens of cooked shrimp dumped at/on the center of its tabletop. The number and size of the shrimp can be chosen by the owner (the table can be filled to the brim, it can hold a sparse offering of shrimp, or can hold any volume in between). A 150 cm baguette should (be custom-ordered to) be used as the sandwich bread for this sandwich. The baguette should be cut in half transversely. Each half then gets attached to the sides of the foosball table as in the above photo. Note that the center segment of each baguette-half should be attached to the shorter of the two foosball table sides, and each of the lateral segments should extend an equal length along each of the table's longer sides. Each baguette-half should roughly conceal the ball-return openings on its side of the table. The shrimp and/or baguettes can be replaced as often as the owner likes.

The third sandwich is a piece of uncooked salmon (filleted is preferable) that's been massaged with an acne cream and then placed between two DVD cases [containing DVDs] of *Cool Hand Luke*. Should the DVD cases "spoil," the case in the above photo is recommended. The salmon can be replaced as often as the owner likes.

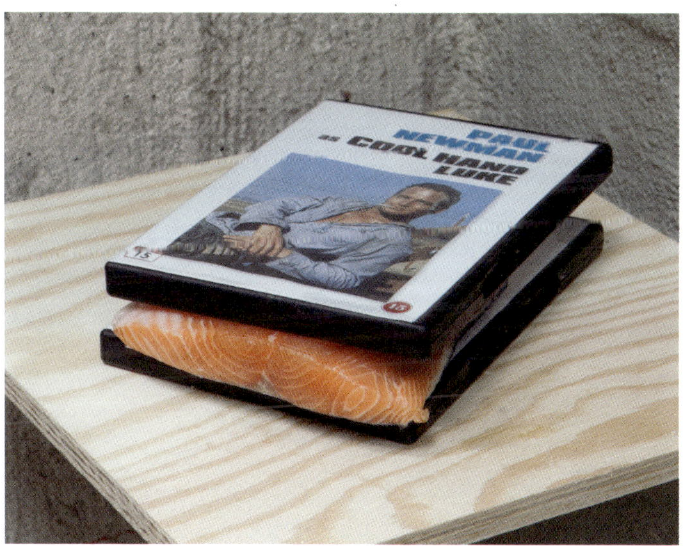

couch; fake couch
dimensions variable
unique

The work consists of: a couch, a fake couch. The couch can be any couch. The fake couch can be any couch. It is somewhat recommended the two have roughly the same amount of seating room. It is highly recommended the two be placed quite near each other—close enough to allow easy conversation between parties seated on opposite/adjacent couches, real or fake.

6⅛ × 8¾ in (15.6 × 22.2 cm)
unique

This work can be displayed however the owner chooses. Of note: the front and back faces of the work are of equal importance; simultaneous visibilty is optimal for presentation.

French horn with/and guacamole (or other "sauce")
dimensions variable*
edition 3 of 3

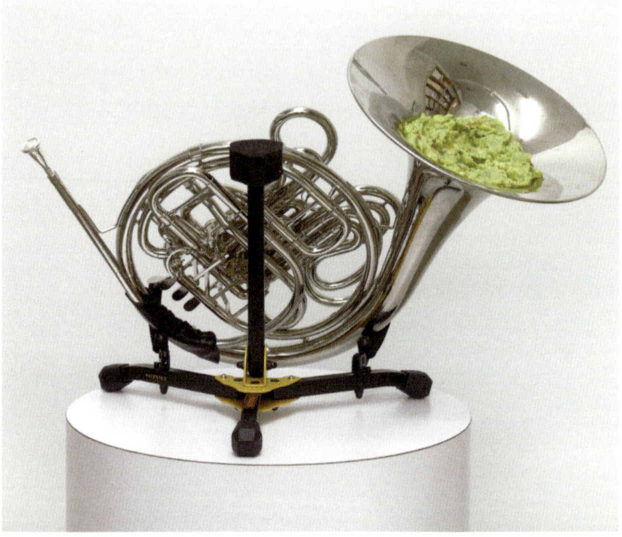

The work consists of a French horn to be used as a serving vessel for types of "sauces." In the above photo the horn is filled with guacamole; other recommended sauces are chunky Italian-style tomato sauce and taramosalata. (If the owner of the horn is feeling adventurous, s/he can try to fill the entirety of the horn with any number of potable liquids.) Although it's fun to use French-horn-with-sauce as a serving vessel, it can also be used for its aesthetic value alone.

The horn comes with a pink rubber plug which is non-toxic. It is recommended that the plug be inserted into the horn's bell prior to putting in the sauce, in order to protect the horn from corrosive agents. A rag can be placed in the horn's bell prior to the plug to absorb any unanticipated leakage. To clean the horn, simply empty the contents and rinse with water and a mild soap. If the horn's brass becomes tarnished overtime, use a brass polishing cloth, or consult a brass instrument specialist. If the owner wishes to replace the French horn, that is certainly ok.

*The horn also comes with a stand and a pedestal; neither of these are necessary for display of the work, although the stand can be quite useful.

clitoris and/with play
dimensions variable
unique

The work consists of two elements: a clitoris, a play. The clitoris can be any clitoris. The play can be any play (although emphasis should be on "play" as noun). The two elements can be any distance apart from one another or in immediate contact. The work can be on/in any surface(s)/space(s). The work needn't be static.

Prototype III, element V.
dimensions variable
unique

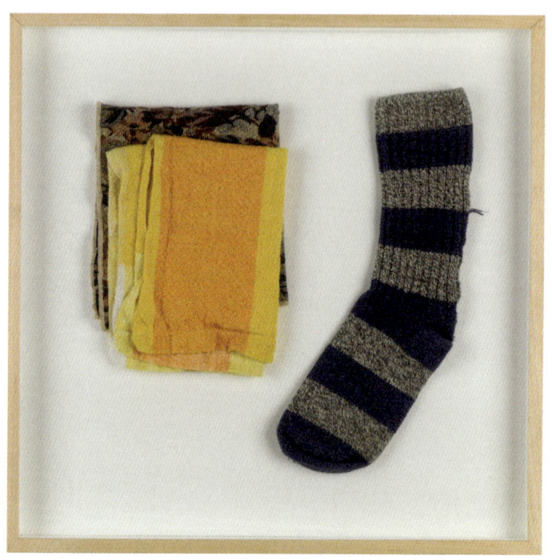

This is element V. [the capital letter, not the Roman numeral] of the work *Prototype III* [which *is* a Roman numeral]. Please refer to your copy of *oaint* to contextualize it in its virtual, textual, and original-spatial environment. If you can't find your copy of *oaint*, n.p.: you can download it for free at www.aaronbader.com/o

The work is known as Artifact 0. [that's a zero]. It consists of two elements: fabric from F.W. Murnau's *The Last Laugh* and a sock of Gerard Adriaan Heineken (cir. 1869). In the above photo the elements are framed together, but it's not required they be framed. If the two elements are not framed, it's highly recommended they remain in close proximity to one another. (The elements should never be framed separately.)

framed printed image
17⅛ × 12½ in (43.5 × 31.8 cm)
AP 2/2, edition of 2

Print: inkjet print on Epson semimatte 260 gsm paper; mounted on Plexiglas. Frame: maple, rag spacer, museum glass.

antipodes group 3: The Four Stations (#1 or #2)
dimensions variable
unique

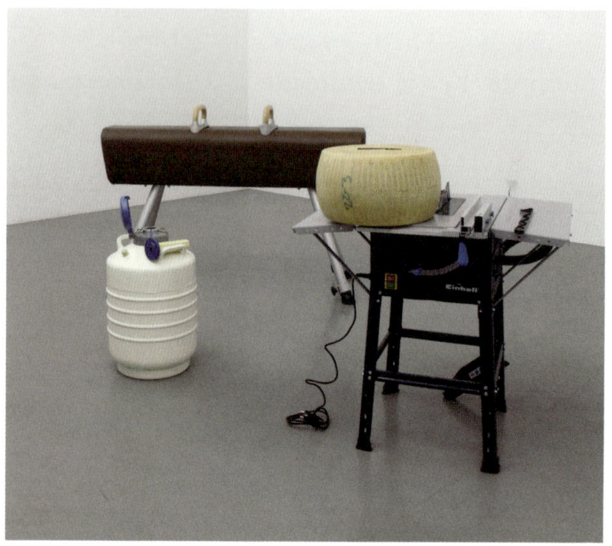

The work is *The Four Stations*:[*] a pommel horse;[**] a cryogenic bull semen tank (that can be filled with champagne and/or decaffeinated coffee and/or Sprite® and/or other potable things someone might want to put inside); a wheel of Parmigiano-Reggiano, "but love observes nuances [invisible] to the indifferent eye, and from them draws infinite consequences –Stendhal" branded on it, resting on a table saw; a cow cared for as follows:

1. S/he should be cared for as if s/he wasn't of any use-value other than as a living being who one cares for as one would care for one's own child, if one was cow:[**] s/he is not to be milked/"milked"; s/he is to be fed well and sheltered comfortably; s/he is to be in the company of other bovines; s/he is to live his/her life out naturally, being afforded all needed veterinary care.[****]

2. When s/he dies, s/he should be buried or cremated (his/her "owner"'s choice). None of his/her parts can be used for human sustenance. None of her/his parts can be used in human-made products.

3. From the day s/he is adopted/purchased until the day s/he dies, she will have a bank account set aside for her/him. The account should always have at least 7,500 USD in it. This money is her/his inheritance when s/he dies. Food/shelter/veterinary/etc. costs cannot be covered by this money. When s/he dies this money will remain in the bank account forever (meaning *at the very least* until the person who has cared for the bovine and managed the bank account has died).

For placement of the work, please refer to the *antipodes* literature on page 2.[†]

[*] Only three of which are in the above photo, the cow being impossible to designate during the work's original presentation. The designation of the cow is incumbent upon the owner of the work.
[**] It's important to mention that the leather of the pommel horse is very likely cow leather.
[***] "...if one was a cow"—indeed this suspends reason to many an extent, but hopefully you understand me.
[****] Veterinary care is clearly not within the bovine ken, but one wouldn't want to see one's child sick or in pain (a human conceit perhaps?); in any case, if the cow is suffering, veterinary care should be employed.

[†]Refer to page 88.

Roe Ethridge
Apple Bees, 2009
C-print
34 × 44 inches (86.36 × 111.76 cm)
Edition 1 of 5

This artwork is a work by Darren Bader. The owner of the above-mentioned framed Roe Ethridge photograph can destroy this certificate to void the artwork's status as a Darren Bader work. If this certificate is destroyed, Darren Bader is unable to guarantee that the resultant artwork will be by Roe Ethridge.

video file
dimensions variable
unique

The work can be viewed/displayed any way the owner would like.

Persian rug and/with tripod and/with sous chef
dimensions variable
unique

The work consists of three elements: a Persian rug, a tripod, a sous chef. The Persian rug can be any Persian rug. The tripod can be any tripod. The sous chef can be any sous chef. The three elements can be any distance from one another or in immediate contact. The work can be on/in any surface(s)/space(s). The work needn't be static.

lasagna on heroin
dimensions variable
unique

The lasagna can be any size/slice/piece the owner chooses. Heroin should be injected into the chosen lasagna regularly. (Since the lasagna is unlikely to "die," dosages are unlikely to require strict monitoring.) Chosen lasagna can be disposed of however often the owner chooses. The work can be placed/kept/taken anywhere.

it seems that I is a false supply – T.S. Eliot
ultimately yours and nothing more
She believed in angels and because she believed in them they existed –Clarice Lispector
We are we not because we choose a community, but because our limits coalesce –Albert Schweitzer
they live
And it makes me feel so sorry
dimensions variable
edition of 1 + 1 AP

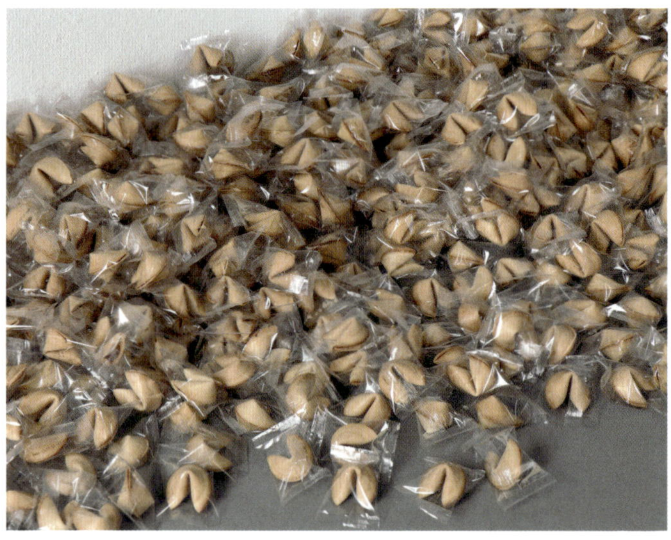

The work is the word-sequence, "it seems that I is a false supply – T.S. Eliot; ultimately yours and nothing more; She believed in angels and because she believed in them they existed –Clarice Lispector; We are we not because we choose a community, but because our limits coalesce –Albert Schweitzer; they live; And it makes me feel so sorry". The work/words can be reproduced in any way imaginable: physically,* vocally, psychically, or otherwise.

*In the above photo, the work/words are contained in a large pile of fortune cookies.

dimensions variable
edition 1 of 2 + 1 AP

The work is a bicycle. The bicycle can be any bicycle. The work can be used however the owner wants.

To Have and to Hold

On the gallery floor are objects.

When any of these objects leave the gallery, the following is prescribed:

1. Live with the object.

2. After a year or so of living with the it, inquire into its origin. This could mean tracing it back to the source(s) of all its component parts*. This could also mean imagining its source(s) as other than those of the physical aggregate achieved by man or nature. Either way, a dedicated inquiry is recommended.

3. Some time after this inquiry into the object's origins—not much longer than 2 years at most—make an effort to collect objects identical** to the object. These should be collected *ad infinitum****.

4. Once a certain, indeterminate quantity of identical objects has been collected, destroy/lose the original object. This is optional (O1).

5. Within 8 years of having begun the collection process, select one of the collected identical objects at random and give that object to someone, telling him/her to copy it within 6 years. Repeat this gift every 6 years, each time to a different person.

6. Every third year, destroy *x* number of the collected identical objects. To determine *x*, blindly choose any number between 1 and *y*. If the number of collected identical objects is less than *y*, they will all be destroyed except one, which will need to be given away. If left with no collected identical objects, begin the cycle again with a new object of your choosing—this is optional (O2).

7. If you die, the number of collected identical objects should not diminish while dead. Any bequests should make note of this. If O2 has been chosen, a bequest can reflect this format.

*This could lead into the infinitesimal, so perhaps it's easier to suggest that its component parts be defined as those immediately perceived by the senses. Language is tricky here since "parts" and "immediately" can easily contradict one another, but the point is to probe as far as one can without need of sensory prosthetics.

** "Identical" is a difficult word. What exactly is identical? It would be tough to prove anything identical. That being said, in collecting identical objects, one should be as exacting as possible.

*** In collecting *ad infinitum*, one should keep in mind that any reproduction of the collected object[s] will undoubtedly adversely affect someone(s) and something(s) somewhere(s).

An explanatory note on the *antipodes* series:

the **antipodes** (pron.: /æn'tɪpediz/ [N.B., phonetic lettering could not be accurately rendered with available fonts]; from Greek ἀντίποδες[1] from anti- "opposed" and pous "foot") of any place on Earth is the point on the Earth's surface which is diametrically opposite to it. Two points that are antipodal (/æn'tipedel/) to each other are connected by a straight line running through the center of the Earth.

The *antipodes* works are most often constituted of four parts/elements (groups of 2, 3, 5, or 6 being uncommon). The *antipodes* works are predicated on the following: the word "antipodes" is not to be taken in its literal sense, but should serve as a guide. The constitutent parts/elements of the work should be dispersed to various parts of the globe. In dispersing each of the 4 parts/elements, one should keep in mind the great distances that separate one part of the Earth from another. In considering distances, one could find that 1400 km separates Berlin from Sarajevo, and this distance is adequate for two of the four parts/elements. But in considering the distance separating the remaining 2 parts/elements, one should make it a point to "scatter" them to more remote loci.

Much like the impossibility of the human eye seeing the entire face of the Earth (even from the vantage of interplanetary space), so the 4 parts/elements should be impossible to see together. (Of course, the Mercator map renders this impossibility possible, but sticking to notions of discrete hemispheres is "of the essence.")

The constituent parts needn't be "permanent residents" of fixed loci. They are quite free to circulate over time, per the parameters mentioned above. They can also reconvene in one place from time to time (a "home for the holidays" type situation).

77 and/or 58 and/with 19

ISBN: 978-0-9906896-3-8

Printed in an edition of 1,000

Primary Information
45 Main Street, Suite 515
Brooklyn, NY 11201
www.primaryinformation.org

Primary Information is a 501(c)(3) non-profit organization that receives generous support through grants from The Andy Warhol Foundation for the Visual Arts, the Graham Foundation for Advanced Studies in the Fine Arts, the Greenwich Collection Ltd, the Foundation for Contemporary Arts, the New York State Council on the Arts, the Stichting Egress Foundation, and individuals worldwide.

Primary Information would like to thank Michael Eby, Elizabeth Karp-Evans, Aaron Kaplan, and Julie Schumacher Grubbs.

Darren Bader would like to thank: "Jesse Willenbring, Owen Kaen, Mariah, Annick, Grady, Lawren, Brinda, Elisa, Sam, Minna, my galleries, the people who have bought my work, my friends."